The Polynesian Triangle

HAWAII

SAMOA

THE MARQUESAS
Veiled by Time

EASTER
ISLAND

TAHITI

THE MARQUESAS

POLYNESIAN CULTURAL CENTER

Text by Rita Ariyoshi

Copyright © 1987 Polynesian Cultural Center

Produced by Sequoia Communications,
Santa Barbara, California

All rights reserved.

This book, or parts thereof,
must not be reproduced in any
form without permissions.

Edited by Nicky Leach
Design by Gay Hagen
Type by TypeStudio
Printed in Japan
ISBN: 0-917859-16-2

Illustration Credits

All photography by Carl Shaneff
except for the following: *Polynesian Cultural
Center by Mike Foley:* Cover, IFC (right photo),
1 (right), 8, 10, 11, 15, 16, 20 (bottom),
21, 27 (top), 29 (bottom), 30, 31, 36 (right),
38, 44 (bottom), 45, IBC; *Rita Ariyoshi:*
IFC (top left), 9, 12, 19 (top), 23 (top),
33 (bottom); *James Ariyoshi:* 34 (bottom), 45
(inset); *Bishop Museum:* 13; *Hawaii Volcanoes
National Park:* 12.
All maps courtesy of the
Polynesian Cultural Center
A special acknowledgement to
Ralph G. Rodgers, Jr. President and General
Manager, Polynesian Cultural Center

Maori dancers demonstrate the art of poi ball twirling during the **This is Polynesia** *evening spectacular.*

A carved wooden ki`i guards the Hawaiian village.

Contents

An Hour's Drive
A New World

One hour and a world apart from Honolulu, the vibrant capital of the United States of America's 50th state, and its glittering international resort, Waikiki, is Hawaii's premier visitor attraction. The Polynesian Cultural Center sits proudly on the magnificent North Shore of the island of Oahu at Laie.

The choice of site is significant. In ancient times, Laie was a *puuhonua*, a place of refuge. A person accused of trespassing against another was given an opportunity to earn forgiveness. He would be released from captivity, and if he made it to the puuhonua before his pursuers, he would make atonement to the priests and be forgiven. Laie was also a sanctuary for women and children during times of war. It is hallowed ground.

Blessed with sunshine, cooled by tradewinds, and tended by patient, hard-working people, this corner of Hawaii duplicates the splendid natural beauty of the scattered homelands of Polynesia.

Defining Polynesia

Eons ago, the great Pacific Ocean erupted in flames — and Polynesia was born. Volcanic sea mounts built these islands, layer upon layer, eruption after eruption, until the gift of land emerged from the depths of the sea. The volcanoes continued their work of creation making mountains high enough to catch the rain clouds —

and even snow. Protective coral reefs formed around the islands. The wind, waves and birds brought seeds and the new land became green.

The oldest of these islands have been reclaimed by the ocean, leaving behind only reefs, a range of atolls, dots of sand. The newest are still being born in flames.

Lava outpourings from these ancient volcanic eruptions have created a dramatic coastline of black rocky promontories invading long stretches of golden sandy beaches. Foam-crested waves endlessly roll in, calling surfers from around the world to test their skills. The North Shore is an area of small towns, banana farms, orchid nurseries, sugar plantations, country people and a way of life still centered around the philosophy of *aloha,* of love and welcoming the stranger. It is an ideal setting in which to celebrate the honored cultures of the many nations of Polynesia.

Two-way Education

In one of the happiest arrangements ever envisioned — and better yet, made into reality — the Polynesian Cultural Center is how thousands of students have worked their way through college.

Getting Started

With missionary zeal and royal pomp, a chapel of The Church of Jesus Christ of Latter Day Saints at Laie was dedicated in 1883. For that occasion, King David Kalakaua sailed with his retinue from Honolulu along the coastline, anchored in Laie Bay and joined the festivities.

The Mormon missionary community experienced initial hardships in farming the barren land and, at times, they held on by faith alone. Once adequate water supplies were discovered, however, the harvests were abundant and the community grew and prospered.

The beautiful white temple that stands at Laie today was built of volcanic rock from Oahu's Koolau mountains, and coral rock from the sea, both pulverized to a fine powder for concrete. This temple, the seventh Mormon temple in the world, was dedicated November 27, 1919.

In 1954, the President of The Church of Jesus Christ of Latter Day Saints, David O. McKay, announced the church's intention to found a college in Hawaii. The following September, 1955, The Church College of Hawaii

Left: A stroll around the Center takes the visitor past cascading waterfalls and brightly-colored flowers and plants. Above: The Mormon Temple at Laie was constructed from volcanic and coral rock and dedicated in 1919.

at Laie welcomed its first 153 students.

Today the 200-acre school is the Hawaii Campus of Brigham Young University in Utah, the largest private denominational school in the United States. It offers a first-class academic and technical curriculum to students from around the world, many of whom could not otherwise afford higher education.

11

The Polynesian Cultural Center emphasizes close relationships between older, respected Polynesian leaders and young students as a way of preserving the Polynesian heritage.

Working Together

The Polynesian Cultural Center has become an environment in which the young people live out the brotherhood embodied in both the Mormon faith and the Polynesian tradition.

Older, respected Polynesians from the various Pacific islands act as leaders and counselors to the students. Believing

that the family is the heart of society, the elders form substitute families with the students who have left their own relatives behind. They share with them an appreciation of their heritage, and as a result the Polynesian villages at the Center are not museums, they are living, vital links to home. They are crucibles of culture.

Helping Preserve Polynesian Heritage

In many areas of the Pacific, the Polynesian way of life has changed dramatically. Not only do the Polynesians often find themselves on the outskirts of the economic mainstream in their own homelands but their ancient culture is in danger of being entirely eclipsed by modern society. These changes have come within living memory of the older generation.

Men and women, the invaluable keepers of tradition, pass on their knowledge, arts, crafts and philosophy to the next generation. The students are nurtured on their heritage while acquiring the education they need for equality in modern society. The Center brings these elements together.

Work is play when it's work that's enjoyed. Obviously, these young people enjoy what they're doing. It's as if they give a party every day (except Sunday, the "Sabbath") and the whole wide world comes. They climb tall coconut palms, break open the fruit and offer it. They teach the hula. They sing, play musical instruments, serve food and answer questions. They are stars and they shine brightly. Their enthusiasm is contagious. They are the primary reason everyone who comes to the Polynesian Cultural Center has such a grand time.

The Polynesians Adventurers of the Pacific

When European sailors first ventured into the Pacific, they were astonished to find a race of people who shared a common culture and similar languages living in isolated island groups scattered across an area larger than Europe and North America combined.

When the British explorer Captain James Cook first sighted Hawaii, he wondered whether these most remote islands were inhabited and wrote in his journal of January 19, 1778, "This doubt was soon cleared up by seeing some canoes coming from off the shore towards the ships...There were three or four men in each and we were agree-ably surprised to find them of the same nation as Otahiete (Tahiti) and the other islands we had visited." In his travels, Cook continued to note the similarities among these greatly separated island people.

A view of Karakakooa in Owhyee (Kealakekua Bay, Hawaii). Engraving after John Webber.

This oil painting by Paul Rockwood depicts what the first Polynesian voyage might have looked like.

The Greatest Story That's Never Been Told

The epic of the Polynesian exploration and colonization of the Pacific is the greatest story that's never been told.

Before the fall of Troy, while Europeans were still hugging their coastlines, afraid they might fall off the face of the flat earth, Polynesian sailors were discovering and charting the vast reaches of the Pacific. Using sophisticated navigational skills employing the sun, moon and stars, the winds, sea birds and the ocean currents, they set sail in huge voyaging canoes, 60 to 80 feet long. Their sails were plaited leaves, the ropes woven of coconut fiber and vines, their charts bits of shell and reed.

These brave men and women established new settlements wherever they went, bringing with them the plants and animals they would need for survival, and the cultural heritage they would pass to their children.

They carefully preserved all this knowledge, their genealogies, the deeds of their heroes and heroines, and their religion, in their chants and dances.

The world, however, did not accept the Polynesians' version of their history because it was not recorded in books. Lacking a written language and due to the ravages a tropical climate inflicts on material objects, there was no real evidence of these epic voyages of exploration. Westerners treated the stories as myth and claimed that the settlement of Polynesia was probably an accident, the result of rafts drifting in currents or fishermen blown to sea in a storm.

The Polynesian Pompeii

In 1981, on the island of Huahine in French Polynesia, archaeologists unearthed a 12-foot steering paddle, a 35-foot mast, huge bailers and planks from a canoe that measured 80 feet long.

Evidence indicated that a tidal wave had hit Huahine a thousand years ago, burying everything in the perfect mixture of sand and silt necessary to preserve the proof of the legends for future generations.

Where the Polynesians originally came from is still a matter of educated speculation. Current theories cite linguistic links to the languages of Southeast Asia. Other historians point to the voyages of Thor Heyerdahl's *Kon Tiki* raft as evidence that the Polynesians first drifted from the Americas. A third group, using agricultural and blood type evidence, maintains that Polynesian roots go back to both continents.

No matter how these adventurers arrived, it is clear that they mastered the ocean. They made it their trade route and peopled a vast area of the Earth.

Following the Canoes Through History

Today in the Carver's Hut at the Polynesian Cultural Center, skilled artisans, using traditional tools, carve beautiful outrigger canoes from huge hardwood logs. The focal point of the Center's Marketplace is the Fijian

This 40-foot camakau or canoe is the focal point in the Center's Market Place. It was carved in the traditional manner by skilled artisans in Fiji and brought to the Center in 1986.

camakau, a 40-foot carved canoe. The fascinating Migrations Museum showcases the epic sea story of Polynesian sailors and their canoes, with charts, displays and artifacts. Visitors to the Center travel the waterways and lagoons by canoe, discovering first one Polynesian village and then another, tracing the centuries-old path of oceanic migrations in less than half an hour. The colorful Pageant of the Long Canoes is enacted every afternoon. Indeed, the canoe is as much a part of the Polynesian Cultural Center experience as it was the focus of life in ancient Polynesia.

Discovering Polynesia in a Day

The distinctive gateway to the Polynesian Cultural Center announces that this is a world apart from its surroundings, isolated, like the Pacific islands themselves.

Students in flowing muumuus and exotic native garb greet visitors, welcoming them as their ancestors did to the special world of Oceania. The spirit of aloha they project is immediate, contagious and genuine.

Stepping up to the box office windows, patrons learn that they are buying an experience — a day and a night in Polynesia, dinner and shows included. Like new arrivals in paradise, they are welcomed, swept up in the fun, and escorted to a day of activity. "This way to the villages of Polynesia."

Hawaii—
An Island in Perpetual Motion

The story of Hawaii is typical of what happened in most of Polynesia. The details differ, but as with other Polynesian cultures, there is more similarity than diversity.

Living for centuries in isolation, the Hawaiians developed a unique culture, in harmony with their limited island environment, ordered a highly structured society of nobility and commoners, and used their religion as a system of law. They cared for their ill with an amazing pharmacoepia of natural ingredients and spiritual self-help, recorded their history in complicated and lyrical chants and dances, and prized both their artists and their artistic expressions in woodwork, tapa (barkcloth) and featherwork.

The impact of the encounter with the rest of the world was immediate and devastating. Within a few years, foreign diseases, to which the Hawaiians had developed no immunities, decimated the population. New plants and animals altered the environment, and their traditional culture was virtually eclipsed.

Thanks to both the steadfastness of people who quietly nurtured aspects of their heritage, and efforts such as that of the Polynesian Cultural Center, there is currently a strong renaissance of Hawaiian culture throughout the Islands. Young people studying their past develop pride in their heritage and face the future with confidence.

Intersecting pathways take the visitor past all the Center's attractions.

Aloha — Welcome to the Hawaiian Village

Fishnets hang drying in the sun beside the lagoon. A waterfall cascades through lush greenery bright with flowers. A carved *ki'i*, or god image, presides over the village, as in ancient times.

Since a Hawaiian family dwelled in many houses rather than just one, the Hawaiian village has a *Hale Noho*, the main family dwelling and a *Hale Mua*, the men's eating house. In ancient times, if the head of the household was a fisherman, there would be a *Hale Wa'a*, a canoe shed, such as the one by the shore of the village, and a *Hale Hoahu*, or fisherman's shed, where he kept his nets and the implements of his trade.

The Hawaiian Village also has a *Hale Ulana*, or weaving hut, where craftsmen perpetuate the art of lauhala work, making lovely baskets, fans and toys. They invite visitors to participate.

At the *Halau*, or house of learning, poi is pounded from the root of the taro plant and served to anyone brave enough to try the notorious Hawaiian staff of life.

Central to the village is the *Hale Ali'i*, or chief's house, and the *Hale papa'a*, his storage house. In reproductions of the impressive garments worn by their ancestors, PCC students explain the significance of the royal jewelry, the beautiful cloaks and the Roman-like helmets. The Hawaiian king and queen are probably some of the most photographed people at the Center, and unlike their stately forebears, invite everyone to pose with them.

Top right: A Hawaiian villager demonstrates net weaving and (below right) a Hawaiian couple show visitors how the hula should be performed.

19

The most famous aspect of Hawaiian culture is the hula, known throughout the world for its graceful movements. "Keep your eyes on the hands," a popular island song goes, and learn Hawaii's story. The hula drums are stored in the *Hale Pahu.* In the shade of a spreading hau tree, hula lessons are taught every day.

To announce the arrival of chiefs, to usher in holidays and begin important ceremonies, the Hawaiians blew into prepared conch shells creating an eerie and commanding sound. The call of the shell is heard again drifting across the village.

There are also demonstrations of Hawaiian throw-net fishing, poi pounding, and fascinating historical lectures.

Above: Both Hawaiian men and women give hula lessons. Below: Pounding taro root into poi is one of the Center's interesting demonstrations. Right: The tall roof of Fiji's Bure Kalou is easily spotted as canoes wind round the waterways.

Fiji—
A Necklace of Island Gems

Fiji is a nation of 322 islands spread like a horseshoe in the blue Pacific embracing the Koro Sea.

The Fijians are the pottery makers of Polynesia. Archaeologists, dating shards of their lapita pottery, estimate the arrival of the first Polynesians in Fiji near 1500 B.C. They were skilled seafarers, builders and weavers of sennit and palm fronds.

European discovery happened gradually, over a period of 300 years beginning in 1643. Captain William Bligh, after his famous mutiny, rowed through the treacherous reef-strewn Fijian waters, recording in his journal all that he observed.

Left: A Fijian "warrior" meets visitors as they cross the bridge to the Fijian village. Right: A lei making demonstration in a Fijian hut.

Fiji's sandalwood forests attracted foreign traders who were followed by Christian missionaries.

To stabilize conditions in their rapidly changing society, the Fijians, under High Chief Cakobau, voluntarily ceded their islands to Great Britain in 1874. British rule continued until independence in 1970.

During the colonial period, the English established cotton and sugar plantations. Finding the Fijians uninterested in their material culture based on wages, the English imported workers from India. Today, people of Indian descent outnumber native Fijians by a small margin, although almost all the land is still controlled by Fijians. Both peoples traditionally practice the unusual rite of fire-walking. The Fijians believe that a legendary spirit god gave the gift to the Sawau tribesmen who live on Beqa Island. When Sawau people walk across the white hot stones, they are acting out their history. Indians of the Madras sect of the Hindu faith practice fire-walking as a form of penance.

Though outnumbered in their homeland, Fijians, with the encouragement of their elders, and through the young people educated at the Polynesian Cultural Center, are saving their arts and beautiful meke (song-dances) for posterity.

Bula Vinaka— Welcome to the Village of Fiji

The tall graceful thatched roof of the Fijian *Bure Kalou*, stands dramatically against the skyline, making the Fijian village the easiest to spot in the Center. People are drawn toward it, crossing one of the bridges leading into the village. There they are greeted by a fierce-looking but friendly Fijian "warrior." They are invited into the Fijian dwellings, their meeting house, their place of work and even their unique retirement home. The house of the chief is distinguished by the cowry shells on the roof.

Twice every afternoon, the Fijian students stage a fashion show, parading the fascinating traditional dress of both men and women of the nobility, the warrior class and common people.

Beside the lagoon, a rope maker practices his ancient craft, weaving from the tough fiber of the coconut, the same type of ropes that held the sails, caught the fish, and lashed the canoes and homes of his ancestors. At the Polynesian Cultural Center, master rope makers, brought from Fiji, continue to teach the young people the honored techniques that might be lost due to the introduction of synthetic fibers.

The Fijians also teach visitors their form of lei making with dried material tinted with natural dyes. There are demonstrations of copra making, again using the bountiful coconut, plus historical lectures, hauntingly beautiful bamboo music, and Fijian dance lessons. Here, you will find a total sharing of the customs and traditions brought from that sprinkling of reef-hugged islands.

Top: Braiding sennit cord.
Below: Bula Vinaka to the Fijian village.

23

Samoa—
The Cradle of Polynesian Culture

Early explorers arrived in the Samoan islands about 1,000 B.C. and became, culturally, the Polynesian people. From there, they set out on further voyages to Tahiti and the Marquesas.

The *fa'a Samoa,* or the Samoan way of life, is still the dominant social force despite the pressures of modern civilization and the fact that the Samoan nation is divided. By treaty with the high chiefs

in 1909, the Stars and Stripes was raised over the part of the island group that is now known as American Samoa. Neighboring Western Samoa is an independent nation. The two Samoas are intimately linked, with families straddling both sides of the international boundary.

In both Samoas, the *matai,* or chief system, is the working social order. With the extended family as its nucleus, it is a pyramidal structure with the village chief administering affairs and making decisions. The family or village chief is responsible to the high chiefs, high talking chiefs and paramount chiefs — more than 8,000 chiefs in all. It is a system of behavior that has functioned well for over a thousand years.

Christianity has been fervently embraced by the Samoans. Prayers are said before every meal and most villages observe a communal prayer time at least once a day. There are more churches per capita than anywhere else in the world. According to a recent Fodor's Guide, "...at least one modern mission, American in origin, gives incomparably more than it receives, tithe-based though it is. That is the Mormon mission." The church has been the agent binding traditional Samoan values of caring with modern social concerns.

The Samoan people live on their verdant, volcanic islands, much as they have for centuries, in open-sided, thatch-roofed *fales,* or oval homes. They have an instinctive joy in life and are often called the Irish of the Pacific. They have also been likened to the Greeks because the Polynesian culture developed its distinctive characteristics here.

Watching the Samoans squeeze milk from the flesh of a coconut is a popular attraction at the Center. Right: This Samoan villager shows lightning skill in climbing a swaying coconut tree in the village.

Talofa—Welcome to the Village of Samoa

No one can climb a coconut tree faster than a Samoan. With exuberant shouts, great wit and the energy of the very young, a Samoan, dressed in lava-lava scales a 40-foot tree as if it were a sandbox toy. He enjoys the cheers and applause, poses among the tree-top coconuts for photographers.

Although no one these days needs to know how to start a fire with two sticks of wood, the Samoans, joking the whole time, show visitors how it is done, quickly. People continue to be absolutely fascinated by one of man's most basic and revolutionary discoveries. Obviously, it is the presentation, rather than what is presented, that draws and holds the crowds.

Fun is foremost at the Samoan village from the guest house to the *Maota Tofa,* the chief's house.

Visitors who begin their tour of the Polynesian Cultural Center in Samoa, learn to weave for themselves a coconut frond sun visor. They will also learn to husk and crack a coconut and to tell the difference between coconut juice and coconut milk. Sampling the delicious nectars is part of the experience.

In the chief's house, there is a lecture, and an opportunity to share in this gentle culture which has so much to teach the world.

Top: The warm smile of this Samoan girl is one of the lasting memories that visitors take with them from the Polynesian Cultural Center. Below: The fine art of making fire fascinates an audience in the Samoan village.

Aotearoa—(New Zealand)
The Land of the Long White Cloud

The first people to arrive at the islands now known as New Zealand were Polynesians who sailed from their ancestral homeland which they called Hawaiki and whose actual location has been lost in time. The first expedition, about 950 A.D. was led by a chief, Kupe, who returned home with precise navigational instructions for reaching the new land, Aotearoa. About 1150 there was another voyage and, finally, in 1350, seven canoes of colonists arrived. Maoris today trace their ancestry to the canoes named Tainui, Te Arawa, Aotea, Tokomaru, Takitimu, Mataatua and Kurahaupo.

Recent archaeological evidence suggests that the Maori found a group of people, the Moriori, also Polynesians, already dwelling in Aotearoa. No one has any idea where they came from, but they were superceded by the more aggressive Maori.

The new home had all the familiar elements of the tropical islands the Maori had left behind, plus alpine mountains, fjords, glaciers, lakes, swift rivers and vast forests. The climate ranged from sub-tropical to temperate.

Adapting to the new conditions, the Maori built homes of timber, became the most skilled woodworkers in Polynesia, and made their clothing of woven flax rather than tree bark.

They developed a tribal society ruled by hereditary chiefs and a powerful priesthood. The tribes became rivals and lived in fortified villages, *pa*, centered around a *marae,* or main courtyard.

Ceremony was, and remains, important to Maori culture and nobody entered a village without elaborate ritual. They developed great oratorical skills and poetic use of language.

New Zealand was discovered by the Dutch explorer Abel Tasman. Europeans came in droves to exploit

Top: *Maori villagers demonstrate ancient battle techniques visitors can learn about in the village of Aotearoa.* Below: *Maori artisans are renowned for their intricate carvings. This master carver demonstrates his skills in the Carvers' Workshop.*

the natural resources. In 1840, the British signed The Treaty of Waitangi with the Maori chiefs, promising to protect their lands from exploitation and making New Zealand a British colony.

Maoris today comprise about 12 percent of the predominantly European population of New Zealand.

Kia Ora—Welcome to the Village of Aotearoa

At the magnificently carved entrance to the Maori stockade, a "warrior" approaches, brandishing his *taiaha* lance, posturing and grimacing menacingly. He places a carving or sprig of greenery at the visitors' feet. If no one retrieves the offering, it means war. If a visitor picks up the sprig, it signifies he comes in peace. He is welcomed and the visit begins.

In one corner of the village, visitors are asked to join in stick games, requiring concentration, coordination and a sense of humor. On the other side of the marae, a beautiful young Maori student teaches poi ball twirling, the unique skill that accompanies so many Maori dances. Outside the **Whare Puni,** or family dwelling, women weave the unusual red, white and black Maori patterns worn by men and women in their clothing. There are lectures on the importance of these patterns and the weaving techniques used to achieve them. There are also lectures on history and the Maori art of tattooing.

Proud of ancient victories, the Maori share their knowledge of weaponry. In

Top: A carved detail on the entrance arch to the village of Aotearoa. Below: A Maori "warrior" challenges new arrivals as they approach the village entrance. This is a time-honored ritual in New Zealand.

a hut beside the lagoon is the carvers' workshop where artisans sculpt and shape wood in the manner of their ancestors. A little farther away is a great war canoe, built to carry 40 warriors to sea — in style. The canoe is not only a maritime marvel, but a work of art.

One of the most stirring experiences of the Maori village is the ceremonial blowing of the *pukaia*, a long slender horn reminiscent of those blown from the towers of ancient European castles.

At the Polynesian Cultural Center, New Zealanders study the honored traditions and learn the fine arts and crafts of the first settlers of their beautiful Land of the Long White Cloud.

The Maori people are known for the intricate patterns used in facial tattoos (now done with makeup), weaving and carving. Below: It's never too early to learn poi ball twirling.

The Marquesas— Veiled by Time

Wild and lonely islands with names like Nuku Hiva, Ua Huka, Hiva Oa are besieged by the ocean and whipped by the wind. Of these 10 islands, only six are inhabited.

The ancient valley people of the Marquesas, separated from each other by mountainous terrain and treacherous seas developed insular little societies, jealous and warlike. Their artwork, particularly in wood, was striking and they left behind beautiful bowls, fan handles, intricate ironwood war clubs and impressive tikis. They also carved massive god images in stone.

It was from these islands that expeditions set forth to colonize Hawaii and Easter Island off the coast of South America.

The islands were discovered by the Spanish in 1595 and named Las Marquesas de Mendoza. Upon approaching the coast, the ship *San Jeronimo* was approached by a fleet of outrigger canoes crewed by 400 men whom the Spanish described as robust, light-skinned with blue tatoos, and wearing their hair long and loose.

Contact was the beginning of the end for the Marquesan people. Foreign diseases, slave raids, the introduction of opium, the continuation of their own warfare and cannibalism killed 95 percent of the population.

The Marquesas Islands are today a part of French Polynesia. Significant archaeological sites at Hane on Ua Huka have shed much light on the mysteries of early Polynesian migrations. Norwegian explorer and anthropologist Thor Heyerdahl lived on Fatu Hiva in 1936 and wrote a book, *Aku Aku*, about his time in this remote place.

*Marquesan wood carving was renowned for its fine detail and beauty. These images guard the **tohua** in the silent village of the Marquesas.*

Ka Oha—Welcome to the Village of the Marquesas

There are no drums here, no dancing. Reflecting the reality of Marquesan culture, this structure is the closest to a museum in the entire Center. Built in the manner of a Marquesan ceremonial compound, or *tohua*, its foundation is Hawaiian coral rather than the basalt rock the

The village of the Marquesas is a silent monument to a lost culture.

Marquesans used in their homeland. The decision to use coral is one the Polynesians would have made, for they were adept at using locally available material. The first Marquesan colonists to arrive in Hawaii undoubtedly improvised the same coral rock for their edifices.

Activities at the Marquesan compound are historical lectures and the sharing of ancient legends. Food demonstrations relate the techniques the Polynesians used to make the most of their limited environment and to prepare food for the long sea voyages. There is an opportunity to sample breadfruit, taro, or boiled green banana.

This village, more than any other, conveys the sense of mystery a traveler often feels when arriving in a strange land.

Tahiti — Beautiful Islands of Mystery

Tahiti is the name of one island in the Society Islands, a group which is part of the vast territory of French Polynesia. Traditionally, Tahiti encompassed the Society group including Moorea, Bora Bora, Raiatea and Huahine.

Current migration theories place the settlement of Tahiti at 300 A.D. when Samoans established the first colonies in the verdant, dramatically beautiful islands. Two centuries later, canoes from Tahiti set out for Hawaii and Easter Island, and in the year 1000 they colonized the Cook Islands and New Zealand.

The Tahitians were ruled by a priestly class headquartered on Raiatea. In 1767, the British ship *Dolphin* sailed into the harbor of Tahiti and hoisted the Union Jack. A year later, the French Captain Bougainville came and claimed the islands for France. With the assistance of European firearms, the Tahitian chiefs of the Pomare clan established their supremacy and ruled until 1880 when King Pomare V signed away his kingdom to France in return for a comfortable pension. The cession

The tamure *or Tahitian version of the hula is a fast-paced, spectacular sight.*

followed decades of political pressure from both France and England.

The pre-history of Tahiti is just beginning to be explored. Vast centers of population existed in the forested mountains. Mysteriously, the people departed their high fortresses, leaving behind foundations of homes, temples and agricultural terraces to be choked by the jungle. Today these settlements are being mapped and researched. Ancient artifacts linking Tahiti with other islands of Polynesia are being examined and categorized. The task is complicated by the fact that nuclear testing in the Pacific has invalidated the radio carbon dating techniques, commonly used to determine antiquity.

The islands of Tahiti range from low coral atolls to the rugged grandeur of Maupiti's sea cliffs and towering green Mount Orohena on Tahiti. Misty waterfalls, bright flowers and turquoise lagoons complete the pictures that French painter Paul Gauguin immortalized in art.

The Polynesians of Tahiti speak both French and Tahitian, and, with the growth of tourism, many also speak English. Thousands of miles away, Tahitian culture is being rediscovered by visitors to the Polynesian Cultural Center.

Iaorana—Welcome to the Village of Tahiti

The drums of Tahiti pound out across the Center, calling, intriguing, luring, as the islands themselves have always done.

Visitors are swept up in the movement, the energy and color of the Tahitian Village. They are dressed in dancing skirts, invited to the *Tahua Orira'a* (dance platform) and taught the exciting Tahitian version of the hula, the one that rocks the palm trees. They

Top: Women in the Tahitian village demonstrate weaving with hibiscus bark. Above: Everyone gets caught up in learning the "hip-shaking dance."

33

are given drums and encouraged to match the boldness of the Tahitians. Everyone joins in. There isn't an idle bystander, not when the air is charged with such excitement.

A plantation at the Tahitian Village grows bananas, enormous papayas, sweet potato, pineapple, and that staple of Tahitian cuisine, breadfruit. At the *Fare Tutu* there is a demonstration of Tahitian cooking and visitors are offered the food cooked in an earth oven.

At the *Fare Ravera'a Ohipa*, women fashion skirts from hibiscus bark, while the men at the *Fare Tautai* mend fishing nets and make marvelous and highly decorative fishing traps. Tahitian crafts, especially beautiful sea shell work, are exhibited at the *Fare Pote'e.*

Above left: Visitors are encouraged to join in drumming along with the Tahitian villagers.

Above: Taro grows abundantly in the plantation near the Tahitian village. Right: There is always something new to taste at the food sampling stand in the Tahitian Village.

34

Above left: Visitors are encouraged to join in drumming along with the Tahitian villagers.

Tonga — The Last Kingdom

Tonga is one of the few countries in the world, and the only one in Polynesia, never to be colonized by a European power. Its royal family, now headed by His Majesty King Taufa'ahau Tupou IV, has been ruling continuously for over a thousand years.

According to Tongan legend, the demigod Maui, who appears in most Polynesian mythology and for whom the Hawaiian island of Maui is named, fished up the Tongan islands from the ocean floor with a Samoan fishhook.

The warriors of Tonga were feared throughout Polynesia and their *kalia*, or canoes, carried their armies to far shores. At one time the empire of the *Tu'i Tonga*, or hereditary king, extended from Rotuma in the west to Niue in the east, and included Samoa.

Today the country is a constitutional monarchy with a parliament. Their laws are based on Christian values with a strict observance of the sabbath that will remind American visitors of quiet Sundays decades ago in small towns. The present king is the son of the beloved Queen Salote who

Young Tongans, dressed in vibrantly-patterned tapa cloth, welcome visitors to the village of Tonga.

Two Tongan villagers proudly display beautifully-crafted tapa cloth. Right: Tapa is made from the bark of the paper mulberry plant. These two wooden paddles help smooth and refine the raw bark.

production. Their tapa cloth, mainly from the island of Tongatapu, is especially notable. All natural dyes are used to achieve the intricate geometric patterns. For both ceremonial and everyday garb, men and women still wear the *ta'ovala,* a mat made of finely woven pandanus leaves and tied as a skirt. The best mats are passed from generation to generation as prized heirlooms.

The islands of Tonga are mainly low-lying atolls with still active volcanoes. The largest building in the island group is the Mormon temple on Tongatapu.

Malo E Lelei—Welcome to the Village of Tonga

The neat, thatched buildings of the Tongan Village are distinguished by their magnificent tapa "wallpaper." These huge sheets of tapa, made from the bark of the paper mulberry plant,

won the hearts of the world when, in a magnificent and typically Tongan gesture of respect, she rode to the coronation of Queen Elizabeth II of England in an open carriage in torrential rain.

Tongan arts are still beautifully hand-crafted without any mass are among the finest examples of this typical Polynesian art.

Young Tongan students, schooled by their elders at the Polynesian Cultural Center in the ways of the centuries-old craft, proudly show visitors how soft, lovely garments are made from the bark of a tree. They also share the dances of their homeland, both the graceful and energetic.

Visitors are challenged to try the seemingly simple game of *lafo,* akin to shuffleboard. They are taught to weave toys from coconut leaves and invited to beat on a Tongan drum with the energy of a warrior. Results can be surprising.

Because Tongans are extremely proud of the stability of their island nation and of their royal family, their village would not be complete without a reminder of royalty. Dominating the complex is a replica of the late Queen Salote's summer home. There is also a **Fale Mohe,** a sleeping house; a **Fale Kautaha,** women's workshop; and the

Above: You can weave a coconut-leaf memento of your visit to PCC in the Tongan village. Left: Tongans have a wonderful sense of humor. These young people are caught sharing a moment of fun at the entrance to the Tongan village.

Fale Fakataha, or village meeting house, where matters of behavior and discipline are discussed and decided.

The Tongan Village is a place to savour Polynesia with those who know the culture best, because even today Tongans still revere centuries-old customs.

Entertainment Polynesian Style

The Pageant of the Long Canoes

Every afternoon the open-air **Hale Aloha Theatre** resounds with music, dancing and laughter. The lagoon serves as a stage with a backdrop of a giant tiki sculpted like the mysterious stone images of far-flung islands.

The Pageant of the Long Canoes is famous throughout the world as visitors to the Polynesian Cultural Center take home tales of this beautifully costumed and most unusual show. The action takes place aboard large canoes that are poled or paddled to their place on the lagoon-stage.

It's a time for offering not only the music and dances of the islands, but for that most respected of Polynesian arts — the sharing of stories. Without a written language, the people kept their history in chants, and in dances they called *hula*, *meke* or *aparima* —the names differed but the purpose was the same — to tell the story of who they

Above: The Hawaiians act out part of the story of Kamehameha the Great.

The Tongans bring the house down with a humorous tale of a young girl's search for "Prince Charming."

The Tahitian legend of Hina and the Eel is enacted by these young islanders.

were and where they originated. Polynesians recorded their genealogies going back as many as hundreds of generations. The kings traced their lineage to the gods. They sang of heroes and gods and danced away the demons. They entertained each other alluding to secret, and often royal, affairs of the heart which could not be mentioned. They celebrated the beauty of creation, practiced for war and wept over losses. They laughed through time and fashioned their dances to the motion of palms in the wind, the rolling of the ocean. Music was the thread binding together the whole tapestry of life and linking past to present.

The canoes begin to sail on stage. The **Maori** present a powerful tale of creation, speaking of the earth mother and the sky father who slept together and begat the race of man. They tell of the time when light first shone in the heavens, and of Tane, the god of the forest.

The laughter is provided by the **Tongans.** With the joy of young love they relate the legend of the daughter of a great chief and her search for "Prince Charming." If there was a roof on the Hale Aloha, the Tongans would bring it down.

From **Tahiti** comes the ancient tale of an eel which falls in love with beautiful Hina, the goddess of the moon, who won't give an eel a second glance. The creature dies of a broken heart and the first coconut tree sprouts from the site.

The **Samoans** enact their time-honored *kava* ceremony and literally rock the boat with their vivacity. Suddenly the surf is up in the peaceful lagoon.

Left and above: The Samoans really "rock the boat" as they enact the kava ceremony.

Below: The Fijians perform a ceremony honoring the high chief.

The **Fijians** portray the reverence and honor they award a high chief, entertaining him, protecting him with mighty spears.

The **Hawaiians** arrive in their war canoes and strange gourd helmets. The famous chief, Kamehameha the Great, is preparing for battle at Waimea. Victorious, he goes to war with the other nearby islands and eventually succeeds in uniting all the islands into the one nation of Hawaii, which flourishes in peace and plenty.

When the last canoe glides away, and the final notes of music fade, it takes a moment to pull back from the enchanted world of legend. It seems that maybe books aren't the best way of keeping the record, after all.

41

Capping It All,
"This is Polynesia" Extravaganza

Ninety minutes packed with Polynesian power, overflowing with aloha and dazzling with color, this is easily the best show in the entire Pacific.

How can it fail with a cast of more than a hundred enthusiastic, talented young performers, towering waterfalls, an "erupting" volcano, and glorious fountains of water.

The entire show was written, designed and directed by Ralph G. Rodgers, Jr., President and General Manager of the Center. With a strong professional theatre background, Rodgers has skillfully merged some of the most beautiful folk music in the world into a thoroughly professional revue. It has heart, meaning and purpose.

The mood is set with the opening *I Sing of Polynesia*, a rich masculine ballad that calls to the heart. The entire beautifully costumed cast from all the nations of Polynesia gathers on stage joining the lead singer, dancing, lending their voices, blending in a picture-perfect tableau of Oceania.

Maori dancing is a dramatic display of movement and gestures guaranteed to entertain the crowd at the Pacific Pavilion.

The lights fade, the cast recedes and suddenly fierce **Maori** warriors, tatooed and terrifying, leap on stage. With their wild gestures, protruding tongues, rolling eyes and strange grimaces they are asking, "Friend or foe?" Tempered by the reactions of another culture, the seemingly comical gestures soften the crowd. They laugh. Friends. The rest of the Maoris enter and sing together in the lilting Maori manner, swinging their amazing poi balls, garbed in their regal native costumes. Maori music is haunting. It leaves people humming, and stays in the heart.

The lyrical mood of the Maori is assaulted by the challenging beat of **Tongan** drums. The atmosphere is charged with tension as a battery of drums vibrate almost to the heavens. Dancers in bright green garb and white feathers perform the Tongan sitting dance, *Ma'ulu'ulu* and the warriors' *Kailao.*

Introduced as a people whose culture stands strong through the winds of change, the **Hawaiians,** gowned in royal purple, and draped with white leis, glide on stage with their gentle hulas. They sing of moonlight and passion, and of the great beauty of their islands and even give the audience a 1940s hula.

The tempo immediately changes with the *Bibi na senico,* the **Fijian** call to battle, as brightly skirted warriors attack the stage, urging their comrades on to greater feats of courage, daring each other, taunting. In the end, dark and shining with exertion, they are united in spirit as they must be in combat. The closing Fijian song celebrates their independence.

The Tongan drummer beats out an irresistible rhythm.

The grace of the Hawaiian hula charms the audience.

The Fijians leap onto the stage and perform a pulse-quickening dance demonstrating warrior pride.

When the **Tahitian** drum beats roll across the theatre it's as if everything up until this point was just an introduction. The Tahitians erupt onto the stage in a splash of color, a loud vivacious torrent of movement. Fountains of pink water shoot skyward, setting the mood for the *Te ote'a mau purotu*, the Tahitian favorite, the dance most associated with Tahiti. The incredible hip movements, the sheer endurance of the women are wonders to behold. The costuming is magnificent with impressive headdresses and thick bark skirts that shake faster and faster when the dancers start moving. The women are joined by the equally enthusiastic men. The Tahitians go out in a burst of glory as the fountains roar skyward in pink geysers, the drumbeats roll across the dark night, and the performers rejoice in the *Hivinau*. As suddenly as they entered the theatre, the Tahitians are gone and the stage is dark.

The festivities don't stop during intermission. Pineapple fruit boats topped with sherbet are sold in the aisles. The songs of the show have been captured on cassette tapes and are available for sale, as are slides for home viewing, a collection of the best of the show by leading photographers.

When the lights come on again, the **Samoans** capture the audience. Their incredible vigor demands attention. Their dances are alternately graceful, comical, daring. In the *Mother's Dance*, older women hilariously teach the younger ones the fine art of flirting. The men do a slap dance — and then there's the fire dance. Dressed in ti-leaf skirts the young men treat fire as a plaything, clowning courageously in the flames. The daughter of a Samoan

This Tahitian dancer is the embodiment of fluid motion.

chief beautifully dances the *Siva Samoa*. The energy is high, the pace changes from moment to moment.

The next segment celebrates Laie as a *Gathering Place* for all Polynesians. The Cultural Center has succeeded in uniting various and scattered groups who were originally one people.

Dramatic Hawaiian *hula kahiko*, the most ancient of the hulas, portrays roots, mysteries. They are dances of Pele, mighty goddess of the volcanoes, and her gentle sister Hiiaka. The chants were once sacred. They are chilling in their primitive force.

The show moves from highlight to highlight and suddenly the stage is ablaze. Samoan men with flaming knives swallow fire, perform amazing feats of courage and daring, as the burning blades fly through the air. It is dazzling to behold.

One hundred strong, the cast comes on stage for a beautiful *I Sing of Polynesia* finale. They're all there, the fierce and the beautiful, in the prime of their lives, happy in having given their best to people who have journeyed from all points of the compass to see them.

These bright young people in their native garb are the hope of their homelands. They have learned well the traditions of their ancestors, and will return with the skills and leadership ability to propel their countries into the future with confidence, integrity —and a pride in who they are and the heritage they carry.

The Samoans amaze the audience with their fire eating and daring feats.

45

Experience the Polynesian Cultural Center

Canoes glide along the canals and lagoons, past the shorelines of Tahiti, Tonga, Hawaii, Samoa and the other proud corners of Polynesia. Well-marked paths meander through the villages, past riots of tropical vegetation, swaying palms and sleepy lagoons. There are maps, signs, and best of all, friendly Polynesian guides to point the way, answer questions, make suggestions and hint at their favorite options — which are probably activities of their own home village.

The sound most commonly heard is laughter. The students enjoy what they are doing. They are witty with the brightness and enthusiasm of youth. They have everyone learning the hula, tasting poi, weaving palm leaves. They entice guests into a Tongan house, where they have their pictures taken with a tall, handsome chief.

But always, there's the beat of a drum around the bend, something else happening. Like the Polynesian voyagers of old, visitors are drawn eagerly onward to the next adventure.

Aside from the seven villages, each with its own distinctive national flavor and full schedule of fun, the Center offers the colorful *Pageant of the Long Canoes* in the *Hale Aloha*. This not-to-be-missed 30-minute show brings to life the legends and customs of the islands in a setting of sparkling waterfalls and floating canoes.

For those in search of new taste experiences, the *Plantation Hut* contains succulent fruits and huge vegetables, nourishing enough to be the staff of life.

In the *Carver's Hut*, proud artisans practice the honored craft of wood carving, essential to the life and artistic

The Center's Market Place offers many handcrafted goods for sale.

expression of Polynesia. Using traditional tools, they work in rare woods such as koa, milo, monkeypod —fashioning canoes and working them to a gleaming silken finish.

Styled on the traditional village markets common throughout Polynesia, the *Market Place* is a center of activity with people making and selling their wares right on the spot. The market is brimming with lauhala baskets, hats

and fans, lovely rare tapa cloth made from tree bark, delicate Tahitian shell leis, Maori poi balls, bolts of bright fabric, hula skirts, carved boats and wooden objects.

More souvenirs, Pacific curios, post-cards, film and sundries are available at the *Shop Polynesia, Hale Kauai* and theater shops.

The *Yoshimura Store* is a typical plantation town store dispensing treats. For generations, Island children have loved "shave ice," frosty cold and dripping with exotic flavor. There's also *Da Kau Kau Snack Bar* and the *Ice Cream Hut* for refreshing tropical macadamia nut ice cream in a pineapple boat, pink guava sherbet, sliced iced pineapple and cold fresh coconut. There are hot dogs and more familiar favorites.

Right in the heart of the Cultural Center, the *Missionary Complex* is a tribute to the selfless lives of the early Christian missionaries in the South Pacific. Built in the 1850s style, which incorporated both elements of American architecture and traditional Polynesian design, the missionary home is a snug shelter hung with magnificent Hawaiian quilts.

Come Along and Learn, If You Wish

The special *Laie Tour* goes beyond the Cultural Center. Aboard a 1906-style Honolulu trolley visitors chug through the historic community of Laie, the sprawling Brigham Young University-Hawaii campus and the beautiful grounds of the Mormon Temple. The free, optional 45-minute tour pauses at the Visitor Center and offers a film and an opportunity to learn more about The Church of Jesus Christ of Latter-day Saints.